Spotlight on Social Justice

CROSSING BORDERS

NAVIGATING IMMIGRATION IN NORTH AMERICA

ELSIE OLSON

TFCB

TWENTY-FIRST CENTURY BOOKS / MINNEAPOLIS

**Dedicated to all the immigrants who
have come before and those still to come.**

Copyright © 2025 by Lerner Publishing Group, Inc.

All rights reserved. International copyright secured. No part of this book may be reproduced, stored in a retrieval system, or transmitted in any form or by any means—electronic, mechanical, photocopying, recording, or otherwise—without the prior written permission of Lerner Publishing Group, Inc., except for the inclusion of brief quotations in an acknowledged review.

Twenty-First Century Books™
An imprint of Lerner Publishing Group, Inc.
241 First Avenue North
Minneapolis, MN 55401 USA

For reading levels and more information, look up this title at www.lernerbooks.com.

Main body text set in Bembo Std Regular
Typeface provided by Monotype Typography.

Library of Congress Cataloging-in-Publication Data

Names: Olson, Elsie, 1986– author.
Title: Crossing borders : navigating immigration in North America / By Elsie Olson.
Description: Minneapolis, MN : Twenty-First Century Books, [2025] | Series: Spotlight on social justice | Includes bibliographical references and index. | Audience: Ages 11–18 | Audience: Grades 7–9 | Summary: "Tens of thousands of immigrants arrive in North America daily, making immigration one of the most widespread-and debated-topics around. Discover the history of immigration to North America and dive into who immigrates there and why, how it impacts the communities they join, and what kinds of legislation and social attitudes affect it"— Provided by publisher.
Identifiers: LCCN 2024009558 (print) | LCCN 2024009559 (ebook) |
 ISBN 9798765627204 (library binding) | ISBN 9798765662588 (paperback) |
 ISBN 9798765659465 (epub)
Subjects: LCSH: Emigration and immigration—History—Juvenile literature. |
 Immigrants—North America—Juvenile literature. | North America—Emigration and immigration—Juvenile literature. | North America—History—Juvenile literature.
Classification: LCC JV6035.046 2025 (print) | LCC JV6035 (ebook) | DDC
 304.8097—dc23/eng/20240403

LC record available at https://lccn.loc.gov/2024009558
LC ebook record available at https://lccn.loc.gov/2024009559

Manufactured in the United States of America
1 – CG – 12/15/24

CONTENTS

INTRODUCTION — 4

CHAPTER ONE
THE FIRST AMERICANS — 6

CHAPTER TWO
COLONIES AND REVOLUTION — 14

CHAPTER THREE
THE NORTHERN EUROPEAN WAVE — 22

CHAPTER FOUR
INDUSTRY AND BOOM TIMES — 30

CHAPTER FIVE
RESTRICTION AND WAR — 36

CHAPTER SIX
REFUGEES AND BRACEROS — 42

CHAPTER SEVEN
THE MODERN ERA — 48

CONCLUSION
A STORY OF IMMIGRANTS — 55

Glossary — 56
Source Notes — 58
Selected Bibliography — 59
Further Information — 60
Index — 62

INTRODUCTION

You've packed all your possessions into two large suitcases. You've said goodbye to family, friends, and even your pet cat. You have no idea when or if you will see any of them ever again. You board a plane and fly for many hours. When you finally land, you cannot read any of the airport's signs. Everyone around you speaks a language you don't understand. The culture and customs feel strange. You step outside, and the weather is like nothing you have experienced before. You take a deep breath. You are just one of thousands of immigrants arriving in North America daily. This is your new home.

People on the Move

Immigrants are people who have left their home countries to settle in a new place. The word *immigrate* focuses on the country where the immigrant is moving to. The word *emigrate* is a little different. It describes someone leaving their current country to move to another. It focuses on the country that the person is leaving. People emigrate for many different reasons. Some seek new opportunities for work or education.

Immigrants play a significant role in the economy of North America. Studies show that immigrants to the US and their children have started 40 percent of *Fortune* 500 companies.

Some flee war, violence, or oppression in their homeland. Many immigrants move to reunite with loved ones already living in different countries.

Regardless of why people choose to emigrate, in their new countries they become part of an enduring human tradition. People have always been and will always be on the move. While immigrants often face challenges in their new homes, they also enrich the culture there. Immigrants bring new ideas, traditions, and customs with them when they move. They help shape the future of their adopted countries. This book will explore how immigrants have shaped North America, especially the United States.

INTRODUCTION

CHAPTER ONE
The First Americans

The first people came to North America at least 16,500 years ago. Most historians and archaeologists believe the first peoples in North America arrived during the most recent ice age, which ended about ten thousand years ago. During this time, Earth's climate was much colder. As much as 8 percent of the planet was covered in ice. Sea levels were also lower, and the North American landscape was very different. Archaeologists aren't sure why early humans chose to migrate. They may have come to North America following food sources, such as large game and fish.

Historians and scientists have several theories about how the first peoples arrived in North America. Many historians believe the first humans arrived on the continent from Asia, crossing a temporary land bridge in what is now the Bering Strait between modern Russia and Alaska. However, spear points found along North America's eastern coast suggest that some early humans may have crossed the Atlantic Ocean from southern France and Spain, arriving in what is now Maryland and Virginia. Another less common theory claims the first Americans crossed the Pacific Ocean from what is now Oceania and Polynesia, arriving by boat to South America's

The Bering Land Bridge is believed to have been about 600 miles (966 km) across at its widest point. The land was a likely a large tundra with some shrubs and trees.

coast. From there, humans made their way north to Central and North America.

Many archaeologists believe multiple theories are true, and that early humans arrived from different places at different times. Once in their new home, these peoples spread out. Within a few thousand years, people populated the entire continent, from the icy Arctic to the warm, wet jungles of Central America.

Vinland Vikings

The Indigenous peoples, descendants of the earliest migrants, were the only people living in North America for thousands of years. These early Americans organized into hundreds of different nations with unique languages, cultures, and traditions. They developed complex agricultural practices and refined hunting and fishing techniques. Indigenous nations built large cities and ceremonial sites. Different nations formed alliances, warred, and traded with one another.

Historians disagree about when the first European immigrants arrived in North America. Viking explorer Leif Erikson likely arrived in what is now Newfoundland, Canada, from Greenland sometime around 1000 CE.

According to ancient Nordic stories, Erikson established a small settlement, which he called Vinland, after the many wild grapes that grew in the area. The people of Vinland traded and later fought with the Indigenous peoples already living there. But the Vinlanders abandoned the settlement just a few years after arriving, returning to Greenland. It would be nearly five hundred years before another European set foot in North America.

Some historians believe Erikson (*left*) arrived in Vinland after sailing off course. Others believe he heard about the land from an Icelandic trader who had seen it from his ship.

Columbus Sets Sail

In 1492 Italian explorer Christopher Columbus embarked on an expedition to sail around the entire world. The king and queen of Spain funded the expedition and hoped to open new trade routes to India. Instead, after several months of sailing, Columbus and his crew arrived in the Caribbean, landing on an island in what is now the Bahamas. The explorers continued their journey westward, landing in Cuba and later Haiti before returning to Spain with news of their travels. The door to North America was open, and Columbus would make three more journeys to the Caribbean before he died in 1506.

Doctrine of Discovery

Soon after Columbus landed in the Caribbean, Spanish leaders worked to ensure this region and all future encountered lands would become Spanish territory. In 1493 Pope Alexander VI issued a decree that helped pave the way for European colonization of North and South America. The decree *Inter Caetera*, known as the Doctrine of Discovery, gave Spain exclusive ownership rights to all land west of Cape Verde and the Azores Islands. This region, which Europeans called the "New World," included North, South, and Central America, and the Caribbean. The document stated that all land in this region was available to be "discovered" and claimed, assuming practicing Christians didn't already occupy it. At the time, most Europeans believed non-Christians weren't human. The document supported the conversion of Indigenous peoples to Catholicism, saying, ". . . the Catholic faith and the Christian religion be exalted and be everywhere increased and spread, that the health of souls be cared for and that barbarous nations be overthrown and brought to the faith itself."

The Doctrine of Discovery was used to justify European colonization of the New World for centuries. Indigenous peoples living in the European-claimed lands had no input on what happened to the lands. Throughout the 1800s the US Supreme Court used the doctrine to support rulings against Indigenous land ownership. The doctrine was cited in a US court case as recently as 2005. In 2023 Pope Francis finally rejected the Doctrine of Discovery, saying, "The Catholic Church therefore repudiates those concepts that fail to recognize the inherent human rights of Indigenous peoples, including what has become known as the legal and political 'doctrine of discovery.'"

Pope Alexander VI

THE FIRST AMERICANS

Columbus's arrival began a wave of European immigration and colonization of North America. In 1493 Columbus founded the settlement of Isabela in what is now the Dominican Republic. Isabela was the first permanent Spanish settlement in North America. While the Spanish colonization of the Caribbean opened new trade routes, it had devastating effects on the Native peoples already living there. On his first day in the Bahamas, Columbus and his men captured and enslaved six Taíno people. He would go on to send thousands more Taíno back to Spain to be enslaved. As Spanish settlements cropped up throughout the Caribbean, thousands more Taíno and other Indigenous peoples were enslaved and forced to work in mines and labor on plantations.

Enslaved Indigenous people who fought back against their enslavement were murdered. Even more died from diseases that the Europeans carried, which the Indigenous people had no natural immunity to. Within sixty years of Columbus's arrival, the Taíno population had dwindled to only a few hundred from as many as 250 thousand. Other Caribbean Indigenous groups, including the Arawak of Puerto Rico and Ciboney of Cuba, were also almost wiped out. Throughout the 1500s Spain's settlements expanded into what is now Florida, Mexico, and Central and South America, devastating the Native populations wherever they went.

The Taíno culture had strong influences on modern Puerto Rican culture. Some Puerto Rican schools introduce students to the Taíno language in order to honor and preserve Taíno culture.

CROSSING BORDERS

In 2018 Los Angeles, California, began hosting an annual Indigenous Peoples' Day celebration. The 2018 event featured art, live music, a powwow, and more.

Honoring History

Columbus Day is a federal holiday in the US, celebrated each October to commemorate Columbus's first landing in the Caribbean. However, many Indigenous Americans argue that the holiday overlooks the impact of colonization on North America's Indigenous peoples. In the 1990s some Americans began replacing Columbus Day with Indigenous Peoples' Day. This holiday honors Native peoples' history and their impact on the United States. Although it is not a federal holiday, more than one dozen states celebrate some form of Indigenous Peoples' Day. In 2021 Joe Biden became the first US president to officially acknowledge the holiday.

Colonial America

By the early 1600s, Spain, Great Britain, and France were fighting for control of North America. Spain claimed the southern portion of North America, including the southeastern and southwestern United States and Mexico. France focused its settlements in central North America, claiming a region that stretched from northern Canada to Louisiana. Great Britain established colonies along North America's northeastern and mid-Atlantic coasts.

Each country had different motivations for colonization. Spain sought to mine valuable minerals, such as gold and silver, and convert Indigenous people to Christianity. French settlers were involved in the fur trade, trapping North American animals and selling their fur to European companies. However, British immigrants established the strongest hold in North America. Rather than exploring or trading, most British colonists were seeking religious freedom and new opportunities in North America. This led to building permanent settlements and creating stable colonial societies.

REFLECT

Some Americans believe the US government should stop celebrating Columbus Day. Do you agree? Why or why not?

Jamestown, the first permanent British colony, was established in 1607 in what is now Virginia. Over the next century, additional British colonies spread up and down the Atlantic coast. Like most European colonists, English settlers negatively impacted the Indigenous peoples already living there. Some colonists formed alliances and established trade relationships with Native peoples. But as more colonists arrived, they pushed Indigenous people off the land they

French colonists often traded with Indigenous peoples, including the Algonquin, Montagnais, and Huron. The French traded iron tools and other goods for furs and canoes.

had inhabited for thousands of years. By the mid-1700s, diseases, warfare, and enslavement had wiped out nearly 90 percent of the Indigenous population in the area that the British colonies occupied.

THE FIRST AMERICANS

CHAPTER TWO
Colonies and Revolution

Many immigrants who arrived in North America during the colonial era, which lasted from the early 1600s to the late 1700s, sought wealth, opportunities, or religious freedom. But not all immigrants during this time came willingly. In August 1619 a ship holding more than twenty enslaved Africans sailed into the British colony of Virginia.

Portuguese merchants had captured the Africans from what is now the West African country of Angola, a Portuguese colony at the time. The small group of Africans had been part of a larger group of about 350 adults and children that Portuguese merchants were bringing to a Spanish colony. There the Africans would be sold as enslaved people. However, before the merchants could reach their destination, British privateers attacked the Portuguese ships. The privateers seized some Africans and brought them to Virginia. There, the privateers sold them to Virginia's governor, George Yeardley.

Conditions on slave ships were crowded, dirty, and suffocating.

Forced Immigrants

The people Yeardley purchased were far from the first enslaved peoples in North America. But these Africans, who had been stolen from their homeland and transported against their will across the world, marked the beginning of the expansive British colonial slave trade. Between 1525 and 1866, more than 12.5 million adults and children were captured, enslaved, and shipped to North and South America and the Caribbean. Most came from West Africa. Only 10.7 million of these people survived the journey.

The British shipped many enslaved Africans to the Americas before slavery was abolished in 1865. However, only a small fraction of enslaved Africans, about 388 thousand, were shipped directly to the British colonies in North America. Most enslaved Africans were shipped to the Caribbean and South America.

"All children borne in this country shall be held bond or free only according to the condition of the mother."
— Virginia law enacted in 1662

The slave trade was part of a three-way "triangular" trade between Europe, Africa, and the Americas. Europe sent guns, cloth, and wine to Africa. Enslaved people from Africa were sent to the Americas. Europe received sugar and tobacco from the Americas.

Indentured Servants

British colonial America had always relied on unpaid labor. Wealthy colonists saw the opportunity to turn the vast amounts of undeveloped land in North America into profitable farms. But first they needed people to work the land.

As many as one-half of early colonists were indentured servants. In exchange for passage to the colonies, indentured servants agreed to work for a wealthy landowner for four to seven years. At the end of their contract, the indentured servants would be free to pursue a life of their own in the colonies.

Indentured servitude was hard, and landowners often treated the servants poorly. But these servants had a promise of freedom to look forward to. Enslaved people were not only enslaved for life, but their children would also be enslaved. By the 1670s slavery had replaced indentured servitude as the primary means of unpaid labor in the British colonies.

There were many indentured servants in Jamestown. Most indentured servants planted and harvested tobacco.

A South Carolina plantation in 1862. Plantations grew crops that owners could sell at a profit. Exploiting the labor of enslaved people made plantations even more profitable.

Fueling Economy and Culture

Enslaved people were shipped throughout the British colonies. In the northern colonies, they worked for blacksmiths, shipbuilders, and as household servants. In the mid-Atlantic and southern colonies, most enslaved people were forced to work on plantations, growing crops such as sugar, rice, tobacco, and later cotton. By 1770 the British colonies had more than 460 thousand enslaved people, making up one-fifth of the colonial population. The newly formed United States banned the slave trade in 1808. But smugglers continued to import enslaved Africans until slavery was outlawed in the 1860s.

Enslaved Africans left a permanent mark on US culture. They brought their music, languages, stories, foods, and other cultural traditions from their homelands. The African diaspora represented many different kingdoms and ethnicities. Once in North America, many of these traditions blended. Black culture was also influenced by European and Indigenous American traditions. The African diaspora can be credited for everything from blues music to hip-hop, foods such as rice and yams, and even influencing the English language.

The Road to Revolution

Slavery was the backbone of the colonial American economy, particularly in the southern colonies. Enslaved Africans and their descendants planted and raised the crops that made white landowners wealthy. As the economy prospered throughout the mid-1700s, new immigrants flooded the colonies, lured by the promise of inexpensive land and work opportunities. Most of these immigrants were British, Irish, or Scottish, but soon Dutch, German, Spanish, Swedish, and Portuguese immigrants also began moving to North America.

The white population also grew as people married and had children. By 1776 colonial America boasted thirteen colonies with a population of more than 2.5 million people, including roughly 450 thousand enslaved Black people. This number did not include the millions of Indigenous Americans who called North America home.

Some arrivals to America in the 1700s were British people who could not pay their debts. Instead of going to prison, they were banished overseas.

By this time, the prosperity and growth of the colonies had begun to worry Great Britain. British King George worked to assert greater control over the colonies. Throughout the 1760s Great Britain passed laws restricting settlement, limiting trade, and introducing new taxes on the colonists. These laws were deeply unpopular, and in 1775 the colonies went to war with Great Britain. In 1776 the American colonies officially declared independence from Great Britain. In 1783 the war ended. The colonies were victorious, and the United States of America was born. Many colonists still loyal to the British king fled the new nation and immigrated to Canada, which was still under British control.

One of the young US government's first actions was establishing laws surrounding immigration and citizenship. Up to the 1760s Great Britain and its colonies were eager to expand America's white population. They had granted citizenship to nearly any European settler who arrived at America's shores. However, now US leaders worked to develop and refine an immigration policy.

Missing Voices

The Americans who led the fight for US independence and organized the new nation's governing principles are often called the Founding Fathers. The government they established and its system of laws are still in use today. However, the Founding Fathers were almost exclusively white men of British descent. No enslaved Africans, Indigenous peoples, or women participated in writing the US Constitution or other early US laws.

The US Naturalization Act

In 1790 the US government passed the US Naturalization Act to determine citizenship requirements for foreign-born Americans. The law declared that any free white immigrant who had lived on US soil for more than two years, along with their children, would be US citizens. Children born abroad to US citizens would also be granted US citizenship. The fledgling US government hoped this law would help rapidly grow the new nation's population. According to the first US secretary of state, Thomas Jefferson, "The present desire of America is to produce rapid population, by as great importations of foreigners as possible."

> **REFLECT**
> **How might the lack of inclusion and representation during the formation of the US government have affected the laws being created, historically and today?**

However, the relatively open-door US citizenship policy did not extend to non-European immigrants or indentured servants. Enslaved and free Black people were not granted full citizenship until the Fourteenth Amendment was ratified in 1868. Native peoples, who had called North America home for thousands of years, were not granted citizenship until 1924.

In 1795 the government limited the Naturalization Act. The changes raised the residency requirements to five years and restricted citizens to individuals of "good moral character." This wording allowed the United States to deny citizenship based on an immigrant's religious beliefs.

The Alien and Sedition Acts

By 1798 the US was on the brink of war with France. The US government passed the Alien and Sedition Acts. These laws were designed to limit free speech and restrict immigration under the guise of tightening national security. The Alien and Sedition Acts allowed the president to arrest, imprison, and deport non-citizens, whom the acts referred to as "aliens," during times of war. The acts also raised residency requirements to gain citizenship to fourteen years.

The US never officially went to war with France. But five years later, in 1803, US president Thomas Jefferson purchased 530 million acres (214 million ha) of French territory for the United States. The Louisiana Purchase, as it was known, doubled the size of the country. Now, the US government just needed people to fill this land, preferably white European immigrants.

The land acquired in the Louisiana Purchase stretched from the Mississippi River in the east to the Rocky Mountains in the west. The land had gold and silver, huge forests, and ample farmland. It would make the US extremely wealthy.

COLONIES AND REVOLUTION

CHAPTER THREE
The Northern European Wave

In 1783 the first US president, George Washington, wrote a letter to recent Irish immigrant Joshua Holmes, saying,

> "The bosom of America is open to receive not only the opulent & respectable Stranger, but the oppressed & persecuted of all Nations & Religions; whom we shall wellcome [sic] to a participation of all our rights & previleges [sic], if by decency & propriety of conduct they appear to merit the enjoyment."

This letter expressed not only Washington's personal views on immigration, but also the early US approach to European immigrants. While some in the US government raised concerns about the impact of immigrants on the new nation's culture, most believed an influx of new people was essential to building the fledgling US economy.

The US welcomed nearly any European immigrant who wanted to make the new nation their home. Despite this open-door policy, relatively few immigrants crossed the Atlantic Ocean before the 1820s. Sailing across the Atlantic

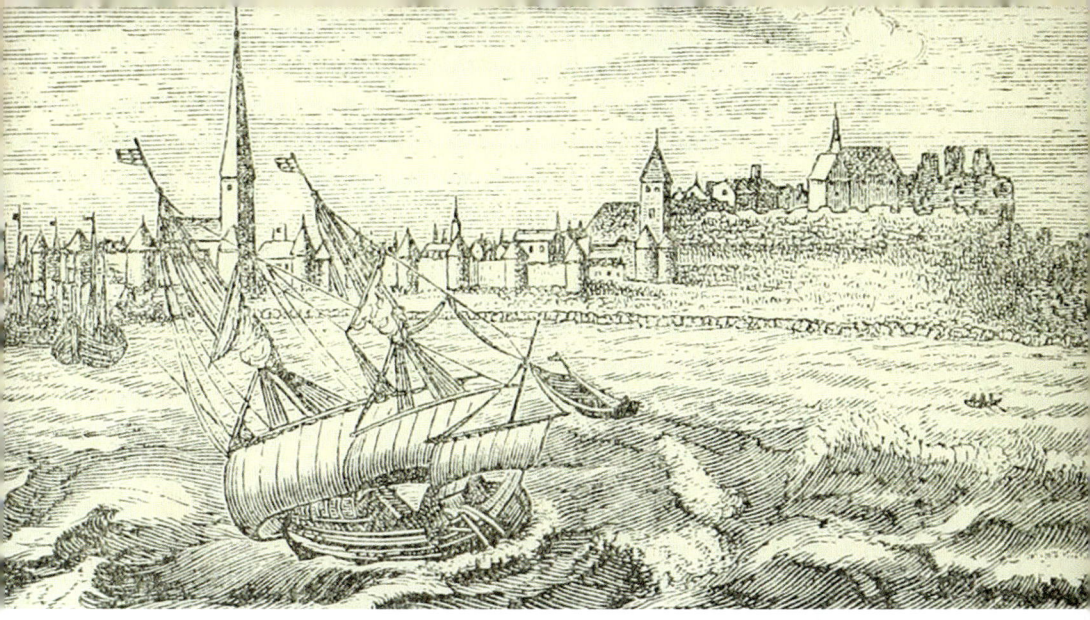

In the early 1800s ships carrying immigrants took about six weeks to cross the Atlantic. In bad weather, the journey could take more than fourteen weeks. When this happened, passengers would often run low on food and water.

had always been a long and dangerous journey. And periods of war between Great Britain and France throughout the early 1800s limited sea voyages. Between 1783 and 1815, approximately 250 thousand immigrants arrived in the United States. Most of these immigrants came from the British Isles and Germany.

A Need for Labor

Because of European wars, the United States had trouble importing the goods Americans needed. The US economy shifted to one that produced and sold its own goods, rather than importing them from elsewhere. But this required more workers. The US did not have enough people to grow crops, raise livestock, work in factories, mine for minerals, and chop timber. Immigrants were the answer to this labor shortage. Most would come from Northern European countries.

Newspapers, posters, and flyers in Northern Europe advertised the US as a welcoming place for immigrants. One British guidebook claimed, "Wages in America are better . . . [more] than in any other country, work can be had." Other prospective immigrants learned about the US from family and friends who had recently emigrated and wrote glowing letters about life in their new home.

Irish Famine

The US demand for workers coincided with increasing economic upheaval and unrest in Northern Europe. Throughout the 1700s Ireland's population had grown faster than any other European nation's. By the 1800s the small country faced overpopulation, which led to scarce resources and work opportunities. The first wave of Irish immigrants were wealthy, middle-class Protestants. But after 1820 more impoverished

Irish immigrants fleeing the famine often carried little with them, having sold most of their valuable possessions back in Ireland. When they arrived in the US, they often sought out churches that offered shelter, food, and guidance to start a new life in a new country.

Catholic immigrants came to Canada and the United States. From 1820 to about 1860, Irish people made up more than one-third of North American immigrants.

Between 1845 and 1852, the potato crop failed in Ireland. Potatoes were the primary source of nutrition for millions of Irish people, particularly for low-income people. The crop failure led to a period of mass starvation known as the Great Famine. More than one million people died of starvation and disease during this period. As a result, many Irish people chose to leave their homes and immigrate to North America. Between 1845 and 1860, approximately 1.7 million Irish immigrants came to the United States and 360 thousand to Canada. Most Irish immigrants settled in eastern cities along the Atlantic Coast.

More Trouble in Europe

Ireland wasn't the only nation affected by the potato crop failure. Many people in western Germany also relied on potatoes as a food source. After the crop's failure, many low-income Germans faced starvation and disease. During the same period, Germany also experienced political unrest as the German people attempted to overturn the monarchy and establish a democracy. Many Germans fled their country during this time, hoping to avoid the unrest and seek new economic opportunities. During the 1800s more than five million Germans immigrated to North America. Most of these German immigrants chose to settle in the United States. Many were farmers who settled in rural Midwestern states. But a steady stream of German immigrants made their way to Canada, settling in the country's vast central plains.

Other European nations also faced unrest during this time. In the late 1700s Poland had been annexed by Russia,

Prussia, and Austria, meaning the country no longer existed. Polish people faced failed revolutions, a lack of work, and discrimination. Between 1850 and 1914, approximately two million Polish immigrants came to the United States, seeking a place to express their culture and Roman Catholic beliefs freely.

Many Polish immigrants settled in large cities throughout the northern United States, such as Chicago, Buffalo, and Pittsburgh. Others formed smaller farming towns throughout the Midwest. Polish immigrants were fiercely protective of their culture. Unlike other immigrant groups at the time, who attempted to assimilate into American culture, Polish immigrants formed and maintained communities that protected their cultural heritage. Many Polish immigrants continued to speak Polish and practice Polish culture long after arriving in North America.

REFLECT

New European immigrants to the United States in the 1800s faced a choice: to assimilate or not to assimilate. What are the implications of choosing to assimilate or not? How might assimilation affect immigrant communities in the short and long terms? If you had to immigrate to another country, would you want to keep your language and traditions?

A Nation Reunited

From 1861 to 1865, the United States was embroiled in the American Civil War, in which the northern Union fought the southern Confederacy. During this time, immigration temporarily slowed. However, immigrants still impacted the war effort. Roughly 25 percent of Union soldiers were recent immigrants. After the South's surrender and the end of the Civil War, immigration numbers accelerated again.

An 1862 US policy designed to promote settlement in the American West helped this increase. The Homestead Act granted 160 acres (65 ha) of publicly owned land to anyone who paid a small fee and cultivated the land within five years. The policy was open to men and women, US citizens, immigrants, and newly freed Black people.

Polish families often worked together on farms. Even children as young as six years old would work from 4:30 a.m. to sunset picking berries or husking corn.

THE NORTHERN EUROPEAN WAVE

The Homestead Act drew new people from Northern Europe, especially Scandinavian immigrants, who were often experienced farmers. Most Scandinavian immigrants arrived from Norway, where they had faced limited agricultural land, resources, and economic opportunities. Between 1866 and 1873, more than 110 thousand Norwegians arrived in the United States. Many settled in the Midwest, building small farming communities. Others traveled farther west to the Pacific Coast, where they worked in the fishing industry.

Meanwhile, the Civil War had devastated the South. Many buildings, towns, and farms lay in ruins. As a result, thousands of white and Black Southerners immigrated to Mexico after the Confederate loss. Many white enslavers moved to Brazil, where the practice of slavery was still legal. More than ten thousand Southerners immigrated to Mexico and Brazil following the Civil War.

The Confederate capital of Richmond, Virginia, was one of the towns badly damaged during the Civil War.

The largest immigrant groups that came through Castle Garden were German, followed by Irish, English, Swedish, Italian, Scottish, Russian, Norwegian, Swiss, and French. About 20 percent of Americans can trace their ancestry to someone who came through Castle Garden.

Castle Garden

In 1850 the US census began collecting data on US immigrants. At the time, 2.2 million people, more than 9 percent of the US population, had been born on foreign soil, and states managed immigration regulation. Most immigrants arrived in New York City, earning it the nickname the Golden Door. In 1855 the state of New York opened Castle Garden on New York's Manhattan Island. Castle Garden was the first official US immigration processing center. There, government officials gathered information about each immigrant, including their age, nationality, language, and religion. The government gave immigrants advice, a place to bathe, and temporary shelter at Castle Garden. One of the main goals of Castle Garden was to protect new immigrants from people who might take advantage of them. Defrauders were eager to cheat new immigrants, promising them jobs and cheap lodging, only to rob the newcomers. From 1855 to 1889, more than eight million immigrants came through Castle Garden. This was 75 percent of all US immigrants during that time period.

CHAPTER FOUR
Industry and Boom Times

Throughout the early and mid-1800s, most US and Canadian immigrants sailed from northern European nations. But as the century ended, the immigrant population was shifting. Between 1880 and 1920, more than twenty-three million immigrants arrived on US shores. Most of these immigrants came from central and southern European nations. The immigrants included Italians, Portuguese, Spaniards, Greeks, Slovenians, Armenians, Jews from Russia, and many others. Most settled in large cities.

At the time, the United States was shifting from an agricultural to an industrial economy. New immigrants often found jobs in the many factories that were beginning to pop up throughout the United States. Many immigrants in this new wave hoped to save money and return to their homelands, rather than making the United States their permanent home. As a result, they were slower to assimilate into American culture than previous waves of immigrants. But most of these immigrants ended up staying.

As North American immigration patterns shifted, so did Americans' and Canadians' views on immigration. This new wave of immigrants was made up of people who often had no

By the 1870s more than 90 percent of immigrants traveled to North America by steamship. The ships were crowded with people and piles of luggage. Rough seas often led to seasickness.

formal education, little money, and spoke little or no English. Many practiced Judaism or Catholicism. These immigrants' cultures and customs were unfamiliar to a US and Canadian population that was primarily white, Protestant, and of Northern European descent. Many of these Americans began questioning whether the newcomers harmed or benefited their country. Some worried about the potential for this new influx of immigrants to influence politics and US culture.

Forming a Community

This shifting attitude toward immigration meant that many newcomers faced discrimination. Immigrants were often victims of xenophobia—the fear or dislike of people from other countries. This led to nativist policies and attitudes, which protected the interests of native-born Americans over immigrants. Stereotypes formed about different groups. Landlords often refused to provide housing to immigrants from certain areas. Some employers refused to hire immigrants from certain nationalities or religions. Other employers took advantage of their immigrant employees, paying them less than US-born workers. Some immigrants were even physically attacked.

Many immigrants responded to this nativism by forming their own communities. Little Italies, Greektowns, and Jewish neighborhoods appeared in cities across the United States. These communities provided safe spaces where new immigrants could experience their homeland's food, language, music, and culture.

Many Italian immigrants settled in New York City near Mulberry Street. They formed Little Italy in the 1870s. Even today, Mulberry Street is lined with Italian restaurants and shops.

Ellis Island and Angel Island

Despite the rampant xenophobia, the US government often tried to make new immigrants feel welcome. In 1886 the Statue of Liberty was installed to greet new immigrants as they sailed into New York.

In 1892 the US government opened its first federal immigration processing center. Previously, states regulated all immigrant processing. The center, known as Ellis Island, was built on an island off the coast of New York City. From 1892 to 1924, more than twelve million immigrants passed through Ellis Island. As much as 40 percent of the current US population has an ancestor who was processed there. Immigrants who passed through Ellis Island could expect a medical examination and questioning. Language interpreters helped ensure all information gathered from immigrants was accurate. Most Ellis Island workers tried to treat the newcomers respectfully. After a few hours on the island, most immigrants were ferried to shore, where they could make their way to their new destinations.

Just like Ellis Island on the East Coast, Angel Island was the main immigration center on the West Coast. Located in the San Francisco Bay, Angel Island was active from 1910 to 1940.

While Ellis Island was mostly welcoming to European immigrants, Angel Island wasn't as friendly, especially to Asian immigrants. Chinese Immigrants faced discrimination under the Chinese Exclusion Act of 1882. Many Chinese immigrants were held at Angel Island for weeks, months, or even years awaiting decisions on their immigrant status. They lived in overcrowded rooms with little privacy and locked doors. They could only go outside if they were supervised by a guard.

Ellis and Angel Islands are remembered as symbols of the hopes and dreams of immigrants coming to America but also the struggles and discrimination many faced along the way.

Asian Immigrants

In the second half of the 1800s, immigrants from Asia began arriving to North America in larger numbers. Most of these immigrants came from China. Between 1849 and 1882, more than 300 thousand Chinese immigrants came to the United States. Most were young men who came to work in the gold mines that had recently been discovered in California and British Columbia. These immigrants hoped to make money to send back to their families in China.

Working on the Railroad

In 1863 construction began on the Transcontinental Railway. This would be the first railroad to connect the east and west coasts of the United States. More than fifteen thousand Chinese immigrants built most of the western half of the railroad. However, their employers treated these immigrants poorly. They paid Chinese workers less than white workers. While white workers slept in train cars, Chinese workers slept in tents. The Chinese workers also had the most difficult and dangerous jobs.

The railroad crossed arid deserts and the Sierra Nevada Mountain Range. Chinese workers labored in extreme heat and freezing cold. They worked in dangerous conditions, blasting rock, digging tunnels, and laying train tracks. More than one thousand Chinese workers died due to the dangerous conditions.

REFLECT

For many years, most Americans overlooked the contribution of the Chinese immigrant workers who built the Transcontinental Railway. Why is it important to learn about the contributions of these immigrants?

The Chinese Exclusion Act

In addition to poor working conditions, Chinese immigrants faced racism and discrimination. Many white Americans felt Chinese immigrants were stealing their jobs. They blamed Chinese immigrants for keeping wages low. As a result, many Chinese-owned businesses were forced to close. Chinese immigrants were often the victims of violent attacks, including lynchings. Law enforcement did little or nothing to stop the persecution.

In 1882 the US government passed the Chinese Exclusion Act. This was the first US immigration law to target a specific ethnic group. It banned any Chinese laborer from entering the United States for ten years. The act also barred Chinese immigrants currently living in the US from becoming citizens. In 1902 the Chinese Exclusion Act was made permanent. During this time, many Chinese immigrants settled in northern Mexico. By 1910 Chinese immigrants were the second largest immigrant group in Mexico. The Chinese Exclusion Act wouldn't be repealed until the 1940s.

Many Chinese immigrants working on the western half of the Transcontinental Railway carved tunnels with chisels and blasting powder through the Sierra Nevada Mountains. They carried debris away using shoulder poles.

INDUSTRY AND BOOM TIMES

CHAPTER FIVE
Restriction and War

As the turn of the century came and went, the push and pull of US reactions to immigration continued. In 1901 anarchist Leon Czolgosz assassinated US president William McKinley. Although Czolgosz had been born in Michigan, his parents were Polish immigrants. The assassination, along with the steady increase in immigrants from Eastern and Southern Europe, caused many Americans to adopt an increasingly nativist attitude.

The US government soon passed the Immigration Act of 1903, also known as the Anarchist Exclusion Act. This law restricted people holding certain political beliefs from moving to the United States. The act also banned individuals who were mentally ill, who had a contagious disease, or who had been charged with a crime from entering the country. In 1907 the act was expanded to ban people who could not work due to a mental or physical disability.

The Dillingham Commission

The nativist pushback on immigration continued, while others argued that immigrant labor was necessary to the US economy.

The US government attempted to find a middle ground between opponents and supporters of immigration. In 1907 Senator William P. Dillingham led a committee studying US immigration. In 1911 the committee, known as the Dillingham Commission, released its findings.

The commission's report was extremely biased and often racist. Its members were largely white men who were anti-immigration. They hoped to prove that Southern and Eastern European immigrants negatively impacted US culture. As a result, the commission's members ignored facts that didn't support their existing prejudices.

The Dillingham Commission Report argued that Northern and Western European immigrants were superior to immigrants from other regions. The report also recommended ways the US government could restrict "undesirable" immigrants. Despite its obvious flaws and prejudices, the Dillingham Commission shaped immigration policy for several decades, drastically reducing the number of immigrants arriving in the US.

The Dillingham Commission

RESTRICTION AND WAR

More Restrictions

The Dillingham Commission's Report paved the way for immigration restrictions targeting specific groups. In 1913 California enacted the Alien Land Law. This law prevented Asian immigrants from owning or leasing land in the state. It specifically targeted Japanese immigrants, who had been arriving in large numbers to the US West Coast since the 1880s. Many of these immigrants had established farms, which meant the act affected their ability to earn a living. Later versions of the law restricted land ownership further, preventing US-born children of Asian immigrants from owning or leasing land.

The Immigration Act of 1917 denied entry to any immigrant over the age of sixteen who could not read at least thirty words in their own language. The act also created a

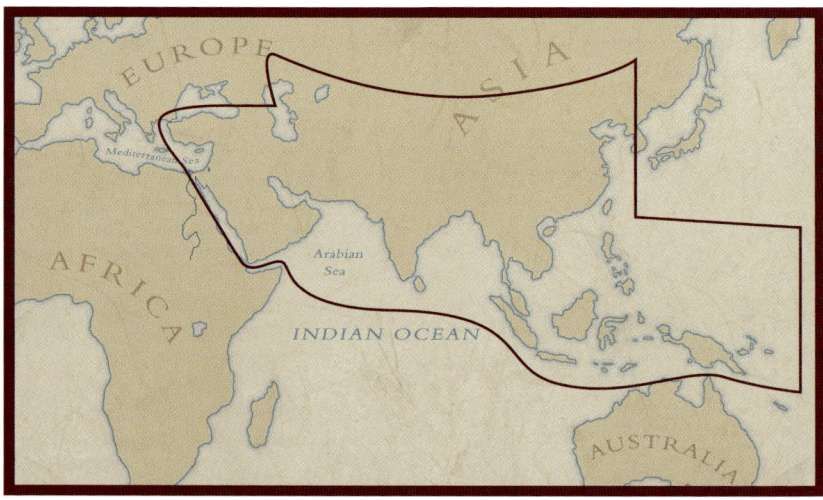

The "barred zone" for the Immigration Act of 1917 restricted immigrants from China, India, Afghanistan, Myanmar, Thailand, parts of Siberia, and the islands of Java, Sumatra, Sri Lanka, Borneo, and New Guinea.

"barred zone" that restricted immigration from any country from a region that included the Middle East and most of Asia.

The Canadian government also took steps to limit unwanted immigration. In 1923 Canada passed a law restricting Chinese immigration. Also known as the Chinese Exclusion Act, the law banned nearly all Chinese immigrants for the next twenty-four years. The law was devastatingly effective. During this period, Canada only allowed between twelve and fifty new Chinese immigrants into the country. The number of Chinese immigrants living in Canada dropped by 25 percent. In 1921 nearly forty thousand people of Chinese descent were living in Canada. By 1951 that number had dropped to just over thirty-two thousand people.

World War I

The Immigration Act of 1917 coincided with the United States entering World War I (1914–1918). The war slowed the number of European immigrants arriving in the United States, and it greatly affected the lives of many recent immigrants already living in the country. When the US joined the war in 1917, the country fought alongside the Allied Powers. This group of countries included France, Great Britain, Italy, Russia, and Japan. The Allies opposed the Central Powers, which included Germany, Austria-Hungary, and Turkey.

The war ushered in a new wave of patriotism and anti-immigrant sentiment, particularly against Germans. More than 2.3 million German immigrants had moved to the United States since 1880. These German Americans now faced harassment, threats, and persecution. Some German immigrants and their descendants even resorted to hiding their German heritage to avoid personal and physical attacks.

The Johnson-Reed Act

World War I ended with the defeat of the Central Powers in 1918. But anti-immigrant sentiment continued to grow across the United States. In 1921 the US government passed the Johnson-Reed Act, which limited immigration to 153,700 people annually. The act also established quotas about how many immigrants could come from each nation. These quotas favored Northern European immigrants from countries such as Great Britain and Ireland. Fewer immigrants were allowed from Southern and Eastern European nations. Asian immigrants were still banned.

World War II

Throughout the 1930s North American immigrant numbers fell even further, thanks to additional restrictions and more global conflict. During this time 50,000 immigrants entered the United States, and 15,000 entered Canada. In 1943 only 24,000 immigrants were admitted to the US and 8,500 to Canada. In 1939 World War II (1939–1945) broke out. This conflict pitted the Allies, which included the US, Canada, France, and the Soviet Union (present-day Russia and fifteen nearby countries including Armenia, Belarus, and Ukraine), against the Axis Powers, which included Germany, Italy, and Japan. As with previous wars, immigrants from the nations opposing the US faced xenophobia, persecution, and mistrust in their adopted home.

About ten thousand people lived in the Manzanar Relocation Center in California during World War II. People had to wait in long lines for food, and they had almost no privacy when using the bathroom or sleeping.

Japanese American Incarceration

In 1941 Japanese forces bombed a US naval base in Pearl Harbor, Hawaii, bringing World War II to US soil. Because of the attack, many Americans began to view immigration as an issue of national security. The US government responded by arresting more than one million immigrants from Axis countries, declaring them to be "potentially dangerous enemy aliens." While some of those arrested included Germans and Italians, the overwhelming majority were Japanese.

In March 1942 the US government began forcibly moving Japanese Americans living on the US West Coast to incarceration camps. These were in remote locations in the American West. The camps functioned like prisons. They were surrounded by barbed wire and guard towers. The living conditions were poor, and medical care was limited.

The US government sent more than 120 thousand Japanese Americans to incarceration camps during World War II. Most of them were US citizens. They often had only a few days to prepare for their incarceration. As a result, many lost their homes, businesses, and possessions. When the camps were finally closed at the war's end, the freed prisoners had to work hard to rebuild their lives.

CHAPTER SIX
Refugees and Braceros

In 1945 the Allies defeated the Axis Powers. World War II was finally over. But the Allies now faced the enormous task of rebuilding countries devastated by the war. This included finding homes for more than 175 million refugees who had been displaced during the conflict. This was the largest refugee population in modern history. In December 1945 US President Harry Truman ordered US immigration officials to prioritize accepting "displaced persons" over other prospective immigrants. However, officials only issued between thirty thousand and forty thousand visas over the next few years.

Denying Refugees

More than six million European Jews were killed during World War II in a genocide that became known as the Holocaust. German chancellor Adolf Hitler led this mission to exterminate all Jews. Many Jews who survived the war had lost everything. They sought new homes elsewhere. But many Americans held antisemitic views. While many Americans disagreed with Hitler's extremist approach, they were reluctant to let Jewish people into the United States.

In 1948 Truman signed a new immigration act known as the Displaced Persons Act. It was meant to make it easier for European World War II refugees, including Jews, to get US visas. However, antisemitism led Congress to build restrictions into the act that limited the number of Jews who could immigrate. Truman himself disliked the bill, saying,

> "The bad points of the bill . . . form a pattern of discrimination and intolerance wholly inconsistent with the American sense of justice.. . . The bill discriminates in callous fashion against displaced persons of the Jewish faith. This brutal fact cannot be obscured . . . ."

Canada's Closed Doors

Canada similarly refused to open its doors to Jewish refugees. Starting back in 1906 and continuing through 1910, the nation passed a series of immigration laws that restricted the immigration of non-white, non-Christian immigrants. Before and during the Holocaust, Canada also created antisemitic immigration laws to keep out Jewish refugees. Canada allowed fewer than five thousand Jewish refugees into the country between 1933 and 1948. This was the smallest number of Jewish refugees admitted among any of the Allied nations. And while many Canadians sympathized with Jewish refugees during World War II and after, the policies remained unchanged for decades.

A New Wave

During World War II, immigration to North America had dropped to its lowest numbers in the last century. But by 1950 those numbers were increasing again. That year Truman signed an amended version of the Displaced Persons Act, which allowed for more refugees and removed the restrictions on Jewish immigrants.

Throughout the 1950s more European refugees sought US visas due to the Cold War—a period of tension between the US and the Soviet Union lasting from the end of World War II through the early 1990s. During the Cold War, US immigration policy focused on accepting refugees fleeing the Soviet Union. By the mid-1970s this included many Soviet Jews fleeing an antisemitic and failing Communist government and society.

The Immigration and Nationality Act

For much of US history, most of the country's immigrants had come from European nations. But in 1965 the US government passed the Immigration and Nationality Act. This act eliminated origin country quotas as well as the ban on Asian immigrants.

Rather than focusing on specific nations, the act created hemispheric preferences. The act allowed 170 thousand immigrants from the Eastern hemisphere and 120 thousand from the Western hemisphere annually. The act also created new categories of immigrants for family members of US citizens and workers in specific professions. These changes opened US immigration to non-European regions, including the Caribbean; Latin America, which includes Mexico and Central and South America; and Asia.

Mexican Immigrants

In the second half of the twentieth century, most immigrants to the US came from Latin America. The majority of these immigrants came from Mexico. But Mexican immigrants had already shaped US history and culture for centuries.

In 1848 the US annexed land that included California, Arizona, New Mexico, and Texas from Mexico. Overnight, more than 75 thousand Mexicans became US citizens. In the early 1900s many Mexican migrants crossed the US border with temporary visas to work as farm laborers. Some stayed in the US permanently. By 1930 more than 639 thousand Mexican immigrants called the US home.

In the early twentieth century, many Mexican immigrants crossed into the US through a border station in El Paso, Texas.

In 1942 the US created the Bracero Program. *Bracero* means "manual laborer" in Spanish. The agreement between the Mexican and US governments allowed Mexican workers to take temporary agricultural jobs in the US. It led to a huge influx of Mexican immigrants. Many Mexicans arrived officially under the Bracero program. But many others crossed the long US–Mexico border unofficially.

Life as a Bracero

Most Bracero Program laborers worked in agriculture or building railroads. However, many employers exploited Braceros. They paid the workers less than US-born workers. The laborers lived and worked in unsanitary and often dangerous conditions. Texas Braceros were treated so poorly that from 1943 to 1947, the Mexican government refused to allow Braceros to work in the state until conditions improved. Employers continued to exploit Mexican laborers after the end of the Bracero Program. Throughout the 1960s and 1970s, many Mexican Americans banded together to protest discrimination, unfair wages, and poor working conditions. Many modern Mexican Americans continue to fight for fair treatment and safer working conditions.

Crossing the Border

The Bracero program ended in 1964, but this did nothing to slow the flow of immigrants crossing the US–Mexico border. In 1986 the US government passed the Immigration Reform and Control Act. This law curbed undocumented immigration while at the same time provided amnesty to the millions of undocumented immigrants already living in the country. Under the law, undocumented immigrants living and working in the US were allowed to apply for green cards and visas. More than three million immigrants received immigration documentation under the act. Most of these immigrants were from Mexico. At the same time, the act discouraged undocumented immigration by penalizing employers who hired undocumented workers.

The Immigration Reform and Control Act increased the number of documented Mexican immigrants in the US. But it did little to slow undocumented immigration. By 1990 more than 4 million documented Mexican immigrants were living in the US, with an additional 2 million undocumented immigrants. By 2002 documented Mexican immigrants had more than doubled to nearly 10 million. An additional 4.8 million were undocumented. The US government attempted to slow undocumented immigration from Mexico with new policies and border security, but none of the measures were effective.

Immigration to Mexico

Unlike its northern neighbors, Mexico has never pursued mass immigration policies to increase its population. But throughout Mexico's history, many immigrants have chosen to make the country their home. From the early 1600s to the 1800s, Mexico was a Spanish colony under European control. During this time, many Spanish immigrants came to the region. In 1821 Mexico gained independence from Spain. Soon after, the country passed its first immigration laws, one being the Imperial Colonization Law. This law allowed Catholics to immigrate to Mexico.

In 1860 Mexico opened its doors to all religions. But immigration numbers remained relatively small compared to its northern neighbors. In recent years, Mexico has become a destination for undocumented immigrants from Central and South America. Many of these immigrants are fleeing political unrest and violence in their homelands.

CHAPTER SEVEN
The Modern Era

On September 11, 2001, a Middle Eastern terrorist group attacked three important US sites by crashing passenger planes into them. Nearly three thousand people died. In response to 9/11, as the attacks became known, the US government began focusing more on national defense and anti-terrorism.

The USA PATRIOT Act

In October 2001 US president George W. Bush signed the Uniting and Strengthening America by Providing Appropriate Tools Required to Intercept and Obstruct Terrorism (USA PATRIOT) Act into law. Among other measures, the USA PATRIOT Act allowed the US government and intelligence agencies to monitor immigrants in a way it hadn't been allowed to before. This included eavesdropping on phone calls, monitoring internet use, and secret videotaping. The act also allowed US law enforcement to arrest and detain immigrants without providing a reason. It made it easier to deport immigrants suspected of terrorism. The act also increased border security measures, including

The 9/11 Memorial is located at the site of the former World Trade Center complex, which was targeted during the attacks. The aftermath of 9/11 fueled a surge of Islamophobia and hate crimes against Muslims across the US.

building more than 800 miles (1,287 km) of fencing along the US-Mexico border and increasing the number of border patrol agents. In 2003 the US government formed the Bureau of Immigration and Customs Enforcement, known as ICE. This agency was charged with enforcing US immigration laws and preventing undocumented border crossings.

Islamophobia

The US government argued that the USA PATRIOT Act would help protect Americans from terrorism. But some people felt the act violated their Constitutional rights. Many worried that the US response to the attacks would lead to discrimination, especially against Muslim immigrants. The terrorists who

REFLECT

Do you think that Islamophobia is still an issue today? Why or why not? Are there other immigrant groups facing xenophobia where you live?

had attacked the United States on September 11 practiced an extreme version of Islam. Although nearly all US Muslims condemned the attacks, they still faced Islamophobia.

Following the attacks, many Americans of Middle Eastern descent were victims of discrimination and harassment. Hundreds of Arab Americans were victims of violent hate crimes, including mosque burnings and physical violence. Under the USA PATRIOT Act, US intelligence agencies spied on mosques and questioned people with Muslim-sounding names. Innocent Muslim Americans were arrested and accused of having ties to terrorist agencies. This racial profiling made many Muslim immigrants distrust the US government.

Changing Patterns

The USA PATRIOT Act and ICE did little to discourage immigration to the US. Between 2000 and 2010, more than fourteen million immigrants made the US their home. This was the highest decade of immigration in US history. Most immigrants came from Latin America. However, an increasing number of immigrants came from Asia and Africa. During this period, Africans were the fastest-growing group of US immigrants.

Many Asian and African immigrants were refugees or relatives of US citizens. About 3.8 million Asian immigrants came to the US during this period. Most came from China, India, and the Philippines. African immigrants came primarily from Nigeria, Ethiopia, Egypt, and Ghana. Like previous groups of immigrants, these groups of African and Asian immigrants often established their own communities in cities around the US.

The Trump administration suspended DACA in 2017. The decision sparked protests around the country. A US Supreme Court decision reinstated DACA in 2020.

DACA

In 2012 US president Barack Obama signed into law a new immigration policy that would change the lives of many young immigrants. The Deferred Action for Childhood Arrivals (DACA) policy allowed undocumented immigrants who had come to the US as children to apply for temporary protection against deportation as well as authorization to work. Any undocumented immigrant under the age of thirty-one who came to the US before June 15, 2007, when they were sixteen or younger, and who had completed or was currently enrolled in high school was eligible. Although DACA didn't grant US citizenship, it allowed thousands of young adults to attend college and start careers without fear of deportation. However in 2023 a Texas judge ruled that DACA was illegal according to the US Constitution. The ruling prevented new applicants from applying for DACA.

THE MODERN ERA

Immigration Pushback

As immigration continued to rise during the 2010s, Americans had mixed views about whether immigration positively impacted the country. As a result, immigration became a central issue of the 2016 US presidential election. Republican candidate Donald Trump took an especially hardline anti-immigration stance, primarily against immigrants of color. Trump falsely accused Mexican immigrants of being criminals. He promised to deport undocumented immigrants. He declared that all Muslim immigrants were potential threats to the US. If elected, Trump promised to build a wall along the length of the US-Mexico border to stop undocumented immigration.

Trump became president in 2017. One of his first acts as president was to pass an executive order that banned immigrants and travelers from specific countries in the Middle East and North Africa from visiting the United States. All seven countries had majority Muslim populations, leading the order to be known as the Muslim Ban.

Trump-Era Immigration

Trump also began enforcing a highly unpopular "zero tolerance" family separation policy. Under the policy, children of undocumented immigrants caught crossing the border would be separated from their parents. The children would be placed under federal care while their parents were sent to jail for entering the country without documentation or at official border crossings.

The Trump administration hoped the policy would deter families from crossing the border. Instead, ICE agents forcibly separated thousands of children from their parents.

Many parents were deported, while their children remained in federal custody. Due to poor record-keeping, it often took months or years for families to be reunited. By the time Trump's successor, Biden, came into office in 2021, more than one-quarter of the detained children still had not been reunited with their families.

> In 2023 a US federal judge approved a ban on the "zero tolerance" separation policy. As a result, the US government could not separate immigrant families at the border for the next eight years.

THE MODERN ERA

COVID-19

Despite Trump's anti-newcomer approach, his presidency had little impact on immigration numbers. During his time in office, he cut documented immigration by about half. However, the number of undocumented immigrants stayed consistent during Trump's time in office. One of the greatest impacts on immigration was the COVID-19 pandemic. During the start of the global outbreak of the coronavirus in 2020, international movement ground to a halt. The number of visas issued to US immigrants dropped to the lowest levels in decades.

The pandemic greatly impacted immigrants in the US. Because of poor working conditions and limited health-care access, people in many immigrant communities were more likely to become sick from COVID-19. Also, many people believed the outbreak began in China. As a result, many Asian Americans experienced harassment, discrimination, and even physical violence. Many US politicians condemned the attacks. In 2021 the US government passed a new law that made it easier to report and prosecute hate crimes.

During the COVID-19 pandemic, some Asian immigrants worried that reporting harassment would cause them to be deported.

CONCLUSION
A Story of Immigrants

Despite the anti-immigrant policies of the Trump Era and the xenophobia of the pandemic, most Americans view immigrants as having a positive impact on American society. When elected in 2020, Biden promised to reopen America's doors. As the pandemic ended, immigration rebounded. By 2022 immigration numbers had recovered to pre-pandemic levels, with more than one million immigrants acquiring US visas. In 2020 most Americans said they believed that immigration benefited their country. They hoped to see immigration numbers stay the same or increase.

The story of North America is a story of immigrants. North American immigrants come from nearly every country worldwide. More than three thousand immigrants arrive in the US and Canada daily, bringing their language, culture, and traditions. From the first Indigenous Americans to new refugees, the United States and North America as a whole have been shaped by the people who came here. Immigrants have helped give the United States the rich and diverse culture it has today, as well as the promise of a bright future.

GLOSSARY

Allied powers: a group of countries (United States, United Kingdom, Soviet Union, China, and France) that worked together during World War II to fight against the Axis powers (Germany, Italy, and Japan)

amnesty: forgiveness given by a country or organization to a group of individuals

anarchist: a person who rebels against any ruling power or established order

annex: to add territory, often by a country

antisemitism: prejudice, discrimination, or hostility directed toward Jewish people based on their religion, ethnicity, or cultural background. A person is antisemitic if they hold prejudiced or discriminatory views against Jewish people based on their religion, ethnicity, or cultural background.

assimilate: to become part of a new culture or society, adopting its customs, traditions, or ways of life

bias: when someone has a preference or prejudice that affects how they think or act, sometimes without even realizing it

colonization: when a country establishes control over a group of people or an area outside its borders. A colony is a settlement that a country establishes outside of its territory.

Communist: describes an economic and political system where property, businesses, and goods are owned and controlled by the government and are available to all people as needed

convert: to change to a new religious belief

cultivate: to prepare and use land for crops or gardening

decree: an official order or decision issued by someone in government

deport: to expel a person from a country

diaspora: the scattering of a group of people who share a common origin, identity, or cultural heritage

discrimination: a prejudiced or biased outlook, action, or treatment

displaced person: an individual who has been forced to leave their home or country due to war, persecution, natural disaster, or other crisis

ethnicity: describes a group that shares similar language, history, and culture but not necessarily a race

expedition: a journey for a specific purpose such as for exploration, scientific research, or adventure

green card: an immigration document that allows a person from a different country to live and work permanently in the United States. This document is usually green in color.

incarceration camp: a facility where people, often in large groups, are detained and held against their will, typically during times of war, conflict, or political unrest

Indigenous: related to the first people to live in a particular place

lynching: an act of putting someone to death, usually by hanging, by a mob of people without a legal trial

nationality: refers to the country where a person lives or was born

nativist: someone who supports or advocates for native-born people of a country, as opposed to immigrants

naturalization: a legal process by which a foreign citizen can have citizenship in a country where they were not born

oppression: unjust or cruel exercise of authority or power

privateer: a privately armed person or ship that is legally allowed to attack or capture other ships

Protestant: a member or follower of a church challenging certain practices of the Catholic Church. They emphasize the authority of the Bible.

racial profiling: authorities targeting individuals for suspicion of a crime or wrongdoing based on their race, ethnicity, or nationality rather than evidence

refugee: a person who flees from their home country to another country to escape danger or persecution

regulation: a rule dealing with details or procedure

xenophobia: a fear or hatred of people from a different country or culture, often leading to discrimination or hostility towards them

SOURCE NOTES

9   "The Catholic faith . . . the faith itself.": "The Doctrine of Discovery, 1493: A Spotlight on a Primary Source by Pope Alexander VI," Gilder Lehrman Institute of American History, accessed February 8, 2024, https://www.gilderlehrman.org/history-resources/spotlight-primary-source/doctrine-discovery-1493.

9   "The Catholic church . . . 'doctrine of discovery.'": Bill Chappell, "The Vatican Repudiates 'Doctrine of Discovery,' Which Was Used to Justify Colonialism," NPR, accessed March 30, 2023, https://www.npr.org/2023/03/30/1167056438/vatican-doctrine-of-discovery-colonialism-indigenous.

15 "All children borne . . . of the mother.": Various, "Colonial Virginia Laws on Slavery and Servitude (1639–1705)," SHEC: Resources for Teachers, accessed February 8, 2024, https://shec.ashp.cuny.edu/items/show/863.

20 "The present desire . . . foreigners as possible.": Andrew M. Baxter and Alex Nowrasteh, "A Brief History of U.S. Immigration Policy from the Colonial Period to the Present Day," Policy Analysis no. 919, Cato Institute, accessed February 8, 2024, https://www.cato.org/policy-analysis/brief-history-us-immigration-policy-colonial-period-present-day.

20 "good moral character.": Ibid.

21 "aliens": "Alien and Sedition Acts (1798)," National Archives and Records Administration, accessed February 8, 2024, https://www.archives.gov/milestone-documents/alien-and-sedition-acts#:~.

22 "The bosom of . . . merit the enjoyment.": "From George Washington to Joshua Holmes, 2 December 1783," Founders Online, National Archives, accessed February 8, 2024, https://founders.archives.gov/documents/Washington/99-01-02-12127.

24 "Wages in America . . . can be had.": Carl J. Bon Tempo and Hasia R. Diner, *Immigration: An American History* (New Haven: London, 2022), 43.

37 "undesirable": Robert F. Zeidel, "A 1911 Report Set America on a Path of Screening out 'Undesirable' Immigrants," *Smithsonian*, accessed February 8, 2024, https://www.smithsonianmag.com/history/1911-report-set-america-on-path-screening-out-undesirable-immigrants-180969636/.

38–39	"barred zone": "Immigration Act of 1917 (Barred Zone Act)," Immigration History, accessed February 8, 2024, https://immigrationhistory.org/item/1917-barred-zone-act/.
41	"potentially dangerous enemy aliens.": "World War II Enemy Alien Control Program Overview," National Archives and Records Administration, accessed February 8, 2024, https://www.archives.gov/research/immigration/enemy-aliens/ww2#.
42	"displaced persons": "The Truman Directive," Harry Truman Library, accessed February 9, 2024, https://www.trumanlibrary.gov/sites/default/files/TrumanDirective.pdf.
43	"the bad points . . . cannot be obscured.": "Statement by the President upon Signing the Displaced Persons Act," Harry Truman Library, accessed February 8, 2024, https://www.trumanlibrary.gov/library/public-papers/142/statement-president-upon-signing-displaced-persons-act.

SELECTED BIBLIOGRAPHY

Baxter, Andrew M., and Alex Nowrasteh. "A Brief History of U.S. Immigration Policy from the Colonial Period to the Present Day." Policy Analysis No. 919. The Cato Institute, August 3, 2021. https://www.cato.org/policy-analysis/brief-history-us-immigration-policy-colonial-period-present-day#voluntary-forced-migration.

Bon Tempo, Carl J., and Hasia R. Diner. *Immigration: An American History*. New Haven, CT: Yale UP, 2022.

Elliot, Mary. "Four Hundred Years after Enslaved Africans Were First Brought to Virginia, Most Americans Still Don't Know the Full Story of Slavery." *New York Times Magazine*, August 19, 2019. https://www.nytimes.com/interactive/2019/08/19/magazine/history-slavery-smithsonian.html.

Montaigne, Fen. "The Fertile Shore." *Smithsonian*, January 2020. https://www.smithsonianmag.com/science-nature/how-humans-came-to-americas-180973739/.

Powell, John. *Encyclopedia of North American Immigration*. New York: Facts on File, 2005.

FURTHER INFORMATION

Books

Cornejo Villavicencio, Karla. *The Undocumented Americans.* New York: One World, 2020.
Written by an undocumented Mexican immigrant under DACA protection, this book tells the stories of undocumented immigrants.

Henzel, Cynthia Kennedy. *US Immigration and Customs Enforcement.* Minneapolis: Essential Library, 2021.
Learn about the history and controversy surrounding the agency responsible for enforcing US immigration laws.

Kamei, Susan H. *When Can We Go Back to America?: Voices of Japanese American Incarceration During World War II.* New York: Simon & Schuster BFYR, 2021.
This narrative history examines the experiences of Japanese Americans, from the attack on Pearl Harbor to Japanese incarceration camps.

Ortiz, Lars. *Walls and Welcome Mats: Immigration and the American Dream.* Minneapolis: Twenty-First Century Books, 2023.
This book examines the ways immigration has shaped the United States, including the history of and current issues surrounding immigration in America.

Yousafzai, Malala. *We Are Displaced: My Journey and Stories of Refugee Girls around the World.* New York: Little Brown and Company, 2019.
Explore the stories of female refugees from around the world, as told by Nobel Peace Prize winner and refugee Malala Yousafzai.

Websites

Chinese Railroad Workers in North America Project
https://web.stanford.edu/group/chineserailroad/cgi-bin/website/
This website, hosted by Stanford University, explores the stories and experiences of the Chinese immigrant workers who built the US Transcontinental Railway.

Destination America
https://www.pbs.org/destinationamerica/index.html
This comprehensive website teaches about the complex history of US immigration, from mass European immigration waves in the 1800s to modern times.

Immigration and Relocation in US History
https://www.loc.gov/classroom-materials/immigration/
The US Library of Congress created this website to explore the immigration stories of various US immigrant communities. Learn who they were, why they came, and where they settled.

¡Presente! Immigration Stories
https://latino.si.edu/exhibitions/presente/immigration-stories
This website from the Smithsonian's National Museum of the American Latino explores the stories and experiences of Latin American immigrants.

The 1619 Project
https://www.nytimes.com/interactive/2019/08/14/magazine/1619-america-slavery.html
This ambitious project aims to reframe US history through the lens of slavery by telling the stories of enslaved Black Americans and exploring how their arrival in colonial America impacted and shaped the United States.

INDEX

Alexander VI (pope), 9
Alien Act, 21
Alien Land Law, 38
Allied Powers (WWI), 39
Allied Powers (WWII), 40, 42–43
American Civil War, 26–28
Americans, 6–13, 17–20, 23,
    29–32, 34–36, 39, 41–42, 46,
    49–50, 52, 54–55
    Arab, 50
    Asian, 54
    German, 39
    Indigenous, 6–13, 17–18, 55
    Japanese, 41
    Mexican, 46
    Muslim, 50
Anarchist Exclusion Act.
    See Immigration Act: of 1903
Angel Island, 33
Axis Powers, 40–42

"barred zone", 38–39
Biden, Joe, 11, 53, 55
braceros, 45–46
Bureau of Immigration and
    Customs Enforcement.
    See ICE
Bush, George W., 48

Castle Garden, 29
Central America, 7, 9–10, 45, 47
Central Powers, 39–40
Chinese Exclusion Act, 33, 35, 39
    of Canada, 39
    of US, 33, 35
citizenship (US), 19–21, 35, 45, 51
Civil War. See American Civil War
Cold War, 44
colonists, 9–19, 47
    British, 12–17, 19

European, 9–10, 12, 19
French, 12–13
Portuguese, 14
Spanish, 9–10, 12, 14, 47
Columbus, Christopher, 8–12

DACA, 51
Deferred Action for Childhood
    Arrivals. See DACA
deportation, 21, 48, 51–54
Dillingham Commission, 36–38
displaced persons, 42–44
Displaced Persons Act, 43–44
Doctrine of Discovery, 9

Ellis Island, 33
enslaved people, 10, 13–20, 28
    African, 14–15, 17–20
    Black, 18, 20
    Indigenous, 10, 13
    Taíno, 10
Erikson, Leif, 8

Francis (pope), 9

Great Famine, The. See Irish
    famine
green card, 46

Hitler, Adolf, 42
Homestead Act, 27–28

ICE, 49–50, 52
immigrants
    Afghan, 38
    African, 50
    Armenian, 30
    Asian, 33–35, 38–40, 44, 50, 54
    British, 12–19, 23–24, 29, 40
    Chinese, 33–35, 38–39, 50
    Dutch, 18
    English, 12, 29
    Filipino (from the Philippines),
        50

French, 12–13, 29
German, 18, 23, 25, 29, 39–41
Greek, 30, 32
Indian (from India), 38, 50
Irish, 18, 22, 24–25, 29, 40
Italian, 29–32, 41
Japanese, 38, 41
Latin American, 44–45, 50
Mexican, 45–47, 52
Muslim, 48–50, 52
Myanma, 38
Norwegian, 28–29
Polish, 26–27, 36
Portuguese, 18, 30
Russian, 29–30, 44
Russian Jews, 30, 44
Scandinavian, 18, 28–29
Scottish, 18, 29
Siberian, 38
Slovenian, 30
Spanish, 18, 30, 47
Swedish, 18, 29
Swiss, 29
Thai, 38
Immigration Act, 36, 38–39
  of 1903, 36
  of 1917, 38–39
Immigration and Nationality Act, 44
Immigration Reform and Control Act, 46–47
immigration (to Canada), 19, 24–25, 39–40, 43, 55
  restrictions, 39, 43
immigration (to Mexico), 28, 35, 47
Imperial Colonization Law, 47
indentured servants, 16, 20
Indigenous peoples, 6–13, 17–19, 55
  Algonquin, 13
  Arawak, 10
  Ciboney, 10
  Huron, 13
  Montagnais, 13
  Taíno, 10
Inter Caetera. *See* Doctrine of Discovery
Irish famine, 24–25
Islamophobia, 49–50

Japanese American incarceration, 41
Jefferson, Thomas, 20–21
Johnson-Reed Act, 40

Louisiana Purchase, 21

Muslim Ban, 52

9/11, 48–50

Obama, Barack, 51

refugees, 42–44, 50, 55
  African, 50
  Asian, 50
  Cold War, 44
  European World War II, 42–43
  Jewish, 42–43

Sedition Act, 21

Transcontinental Railway, 34–35
Truman, Harry, 42–44
Trump, Donald, 51–55

USA PATRIOT Act, 48–50
US Naturalization Act, 20

visas, 42–46, 54–55

Washington, George, 22
World War I, 39–40
World War II, 40–44

xenophobia, 31–33, 40, 49, 55

"zero tolerance" (family separation policy), 52–53

63

ABOUT THE AUTHOR

Elsie Olson is a writer from Minnetrista, Minnesota. She has written many fiction and nonfiction books for young readers. Her areas of expertise include science and history. When not writing, she enjoys gardening, trail running, cross-country skiing, and spending time with her family.

PHOTO ACKNOWLEDGMENTS

The images in this book are used with the permission of: © New Africa/Adobe Stock, p. 5; © Gary Hincks/Science Source, p. 7; © Hans Dahl/Wikimedia Commons, p. 8; © Pedro Berruguete/Wikimedia Commons, p. 9; © Danica Coto/AP Images, p. 10; © Luke Harold/Flickr, p. 11; © Library of Congress, pp. 13, 14, 17, 24, 27, 28, 29, 31, 32, 35, 37, 41, 45; © rtguest/iStockphoto, pp. 15, 38 (base maps); © Science Source, p. 16; © Everett Collection Inc/Alamy Photo, p. 18; © Jose Gil/Adobe Stock, p. 21; © The Reading Room/Alamy Photo, p. 23; © Francois Roux/Shutterstock Images, p. 49; © Sheila Fitzgerald/Shutterstock Images, p. 51; © soupstock/Adobe Stock, p. 53; © Anna/Adobe Stock, p. 54.

Cover Photo: © robsonphoto/Adobe Stock

Design Elements: © Ezhevika/Shutterstock Images